COMPOSER
SHOWCASE
HAL LEONARD
STUDENT PIANO LIBRARY

Big Apple Jazz

EIGHT ORIGINAL PIANO SOLOS

BY JEREMY SISKIND

CONTENTS

ISBN 978-1-5400-2956-0

HAL•LEONARD®

Visit Hal Leonard Online at
www.halleonard.com

Contact Us:
Hal Leonard
7777 West Bluemound Road
Milwaukee, WI 53213
Email: info@halleonard.com

In Europe contact:
Hal Leonard Europe Limited
Distribution Centre, Newmarket Road
Bury St Edmunds, Suffolk, IP33 3YB
Email: info@halleonardeurope.com

In Australia contact:
Hal Leonard Australia Pty. Ltd.
4 Lentara Court
Cheltenham, Victoria, 3192 Australia
Email: info@halleonard.com.au

Composer's Notes

Although I haven't lived there for many years now, New York City is still the place where I feel most at home. I love the bustling streets, the people from all backgrounds, the manic energy, the roar of the subways, and the glamour of Broadway. Sure, it's a little dirty, a little smelly, a little crowded, and the people can be a little rude, but there's nothing as magical to me as a fall day in Central Park or a summer night in Greenwich Village. I hope that these pieces share a little bit of the magic of New York with you… without any of the rats!

–Jeremy Siskind

Bronx Accent

People in the Bronx are known for being tough and maybe a little rough around the edges. This piece portrays that Bronx attitude, so make sure to play with rhythmic precision and a strong commitment to the articulation, especially the accents.

Brooklyn Sunset

Imagine that it's 7:30 PM on a summer's day and you're walking to the Brooklyn Bridge. Skyscrapers are gleaming with the evening's last pink light and the water where the rivers meet glimmers in front of you. You can spot the Statue of Liberty on Ellis Island out in the distance and the towering steel buildings of Wall Street ahead. That's the feeling "Brooklyn Sunset" is hoping to capture. You can play this piece with a little bit of a sway, an underlying feeling of nostalgia. Enjoy the colorful harmonies!

Harlem Tapdance

Harlem is the traditional center of African American culture—great African American poets, musicians, and dancers all called Harlem home. When I think of Harlem, I can't help but think of one of my favorite pianists, Thelonious Monk, who was the house pianist at Minton's Playhouse in Harlem. This piece features some of Monk's signature style of "angular" melodies and dissonant harmonies. Don't be afraid of the dissonances—they won't sound pretty, but they should sound cool! Snap your fingers where it's marked to "snap" in the music.

Immigrant's Song

New York has always been the hub for new Americans arriving from Europe. The presence of a large immigrant population makes the city (and the country) unique. In fact, my ancestors arrived many years ago by way of Ellis Island. This piece has an Eastern European elegance that hopes to capture the songs and culture so many immigrants brought with them on their long journeys to America.

Late Night Subway Platform

The subway is where everyone meets—the rich, the poor, artists, and businessmen all converge underground to go careening across the city in high-speed trains. If you're taking the subway after midnight, though, the platforms can be deserted and a little ominous. If you think about men in trench coats swapping briefcases in film noir movies you'll have the right idea for this piece!

Puerto Rican Day Parade

The energetic Hispanic cultures that are prevalent in New York add spice to the city's culture. Their food, language, and attitude are defining attributes of many of the city's neighborhoods like Washington Heights and Spanish Harlem. One annual cultural highlight is the Puerto Rican Day Parade, a summer event that features a display of best music, dancing, and food of Puerto Rico. Pay attention to the difficult rhythm of this piece and don't forget to tap your foot on beats one and three to keep track of the downbeat!

Skyscraper

When you live in New York, it's easy to become accustomed to walking among giants—on nearly every block there are buildings that reach high into the clouds. But every once in a while, even the most jaded New Yorker cranes up her neck and fills with awe at the sheer height of these behemoths! This piece is meant to express that awe and can be played with lots of rhythmic freedom.

Upper East Side

The Upper East Side is where New York's "old money" lives. The neighborhood is very "hoity-toity," that is, wealthy and not afraid to show it! The piece, "Upper East Side," is meant to sound like a "businessman's bounce," a jazz term for groovy-but-not-edgy music like that made famous by Frank Sinatra.

Immigrant's Song

(for Ellis Island)

By Jeremy Siskind

With wonder (not too slow) (♩ = 110)

pp

una corda; use damper pedal as needed

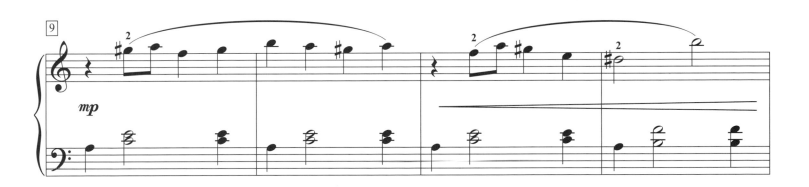

To Coda ⊕

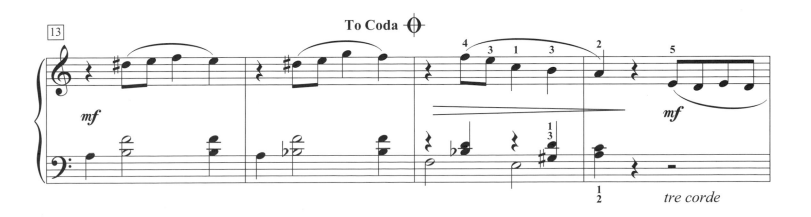

tre corde

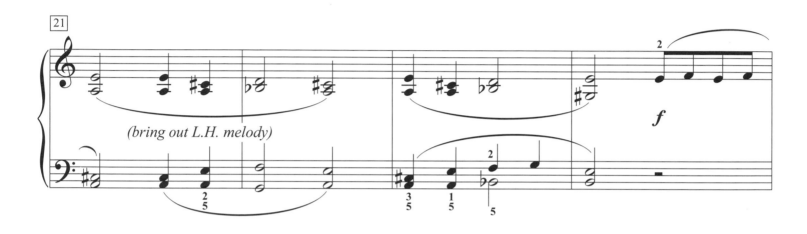

(bring out L.H. melody)

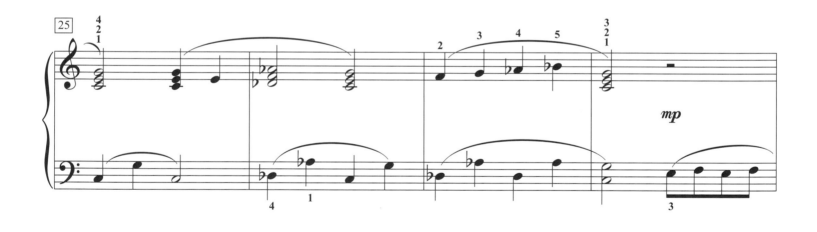

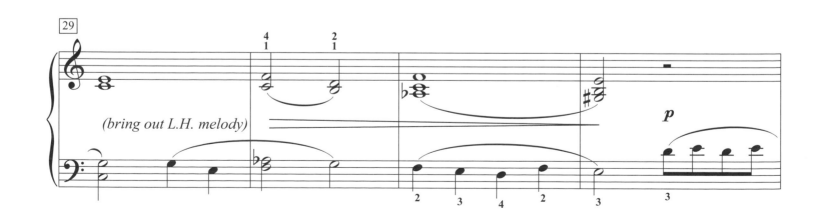

(bring out L.H. melody)

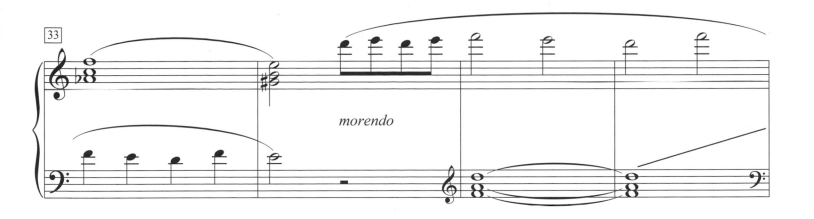

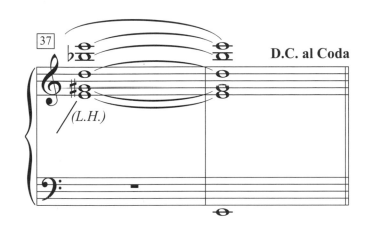

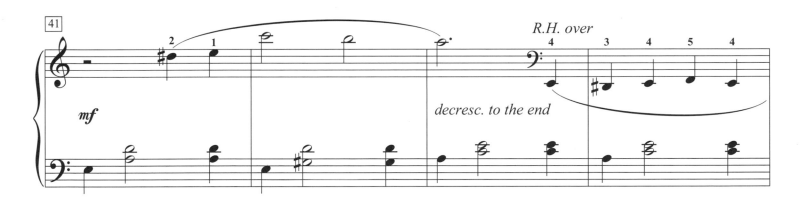

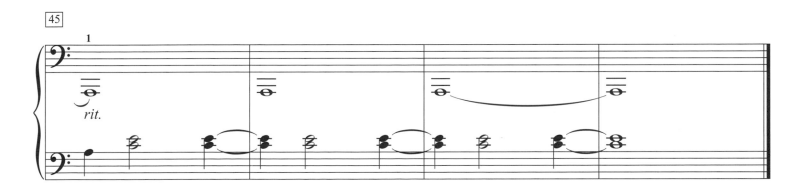

Bronx Accent

By Jeremy Siskind

Swing, with attitude (♩ = 76)

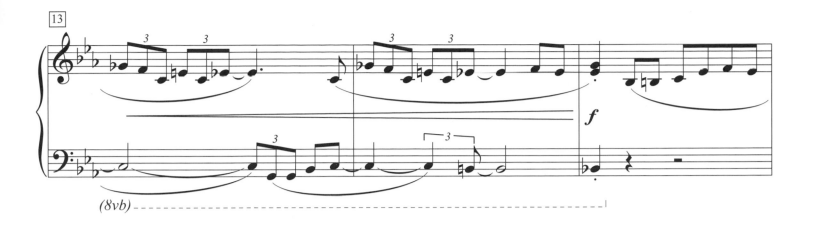

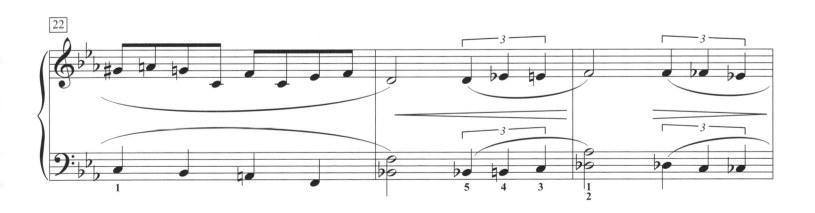

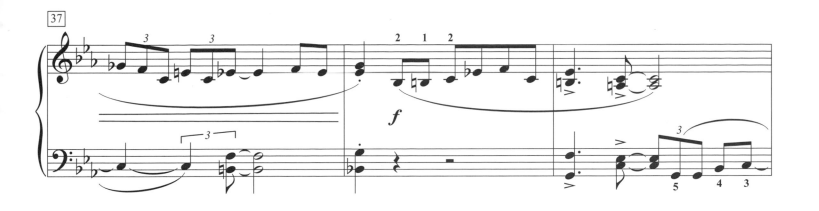

Brooklyn Sunset

By Jeremy Siskind

Brisk, flowing Waltz (♩ = 144)

With pedal

To Coda

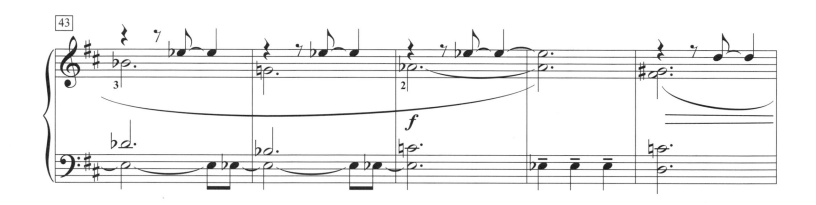

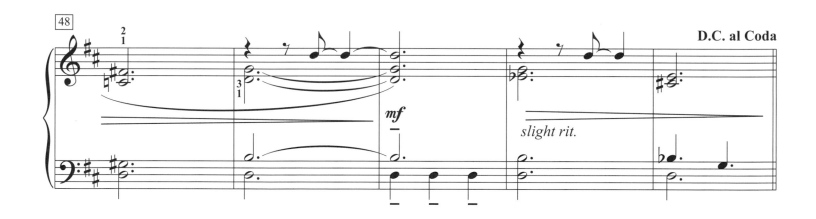

12

Harlem Tapdance

By Jeremy Siskind

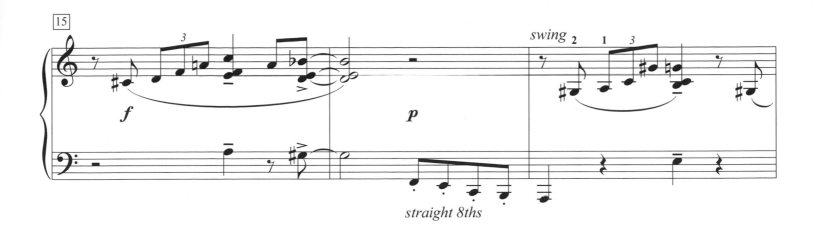

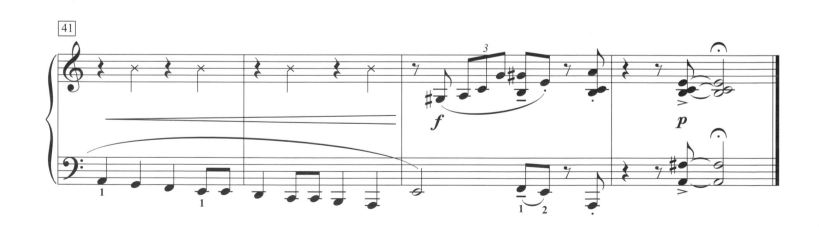

Late Night Subway Platform

By Jeremy Siskind

Slinky medium-slow Swing (♩ = 96)

Puerto Rican Day Parade

By Jeremy Siskind

Upper East Side

By Jeremy Siskind

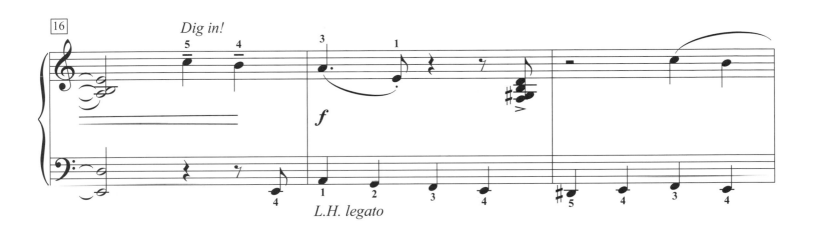

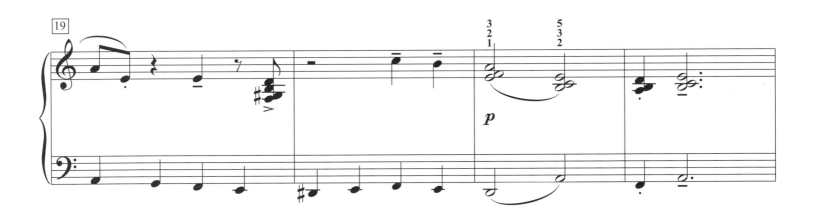

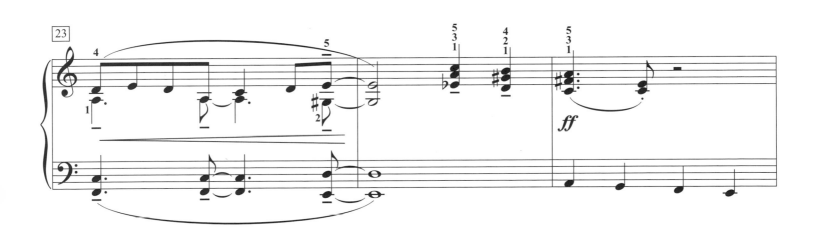

Skyscraper

By Jeremy Siskind

Swift rubato, with awe (♩ = 124)

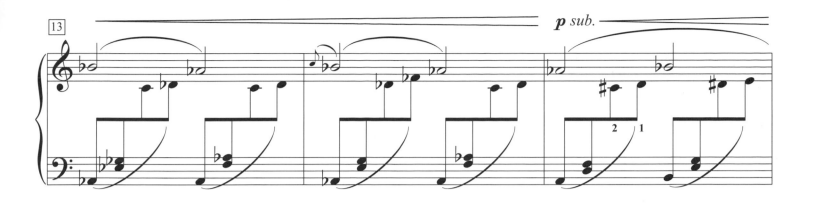

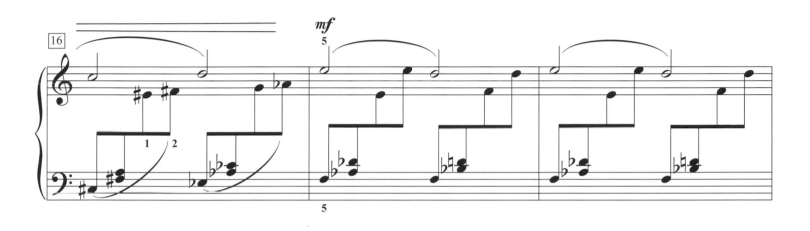

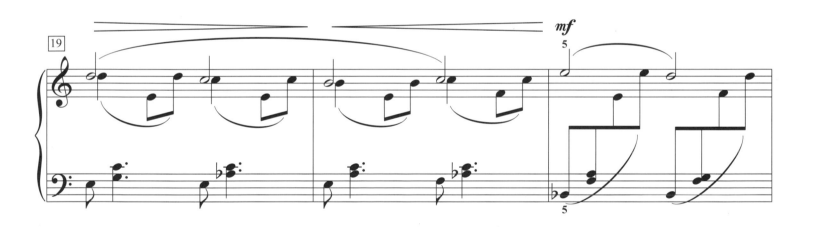

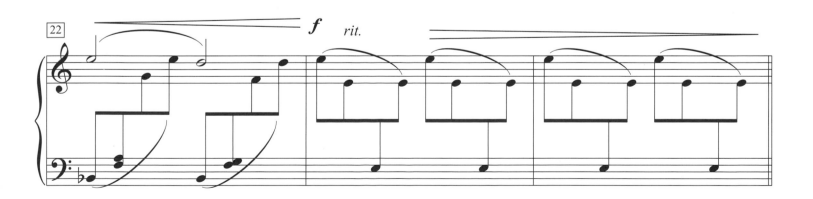

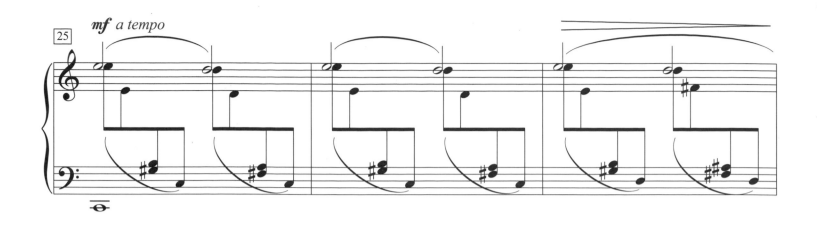

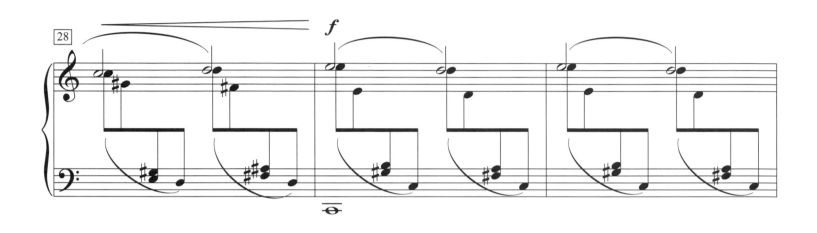

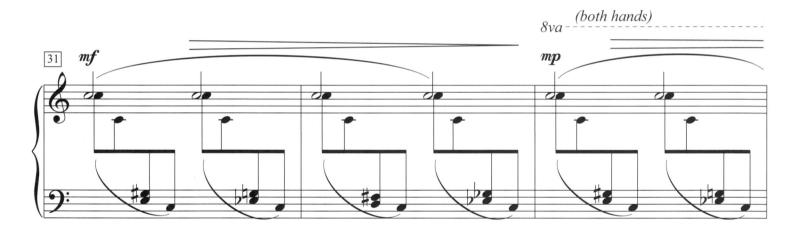

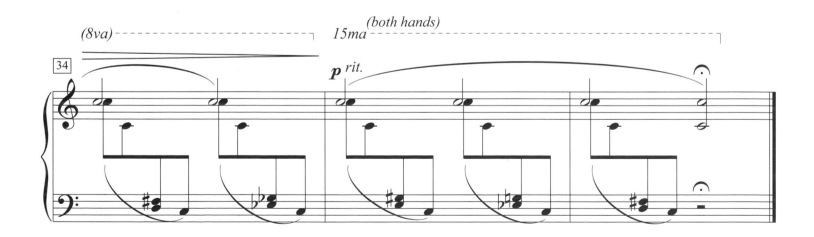